Cavachons

by Ruth Owen

PowerKiDS press

New York

Published in 2013 by The Rosen Publishing Group, Inc.
29 East 21st Street, New York, NY 10010

First Edition

Produced for Rosen by Ruby Tuesday Books Ltd
Editor for Ruby Tuesday Books Ltd: Mark J. Sachner
US Editor: Sara Antill
Designer: Emma Randall

Photo Credits:
Cover, 1, 3, 4–5, 6–7, 8–9, 10–11, 12, 14–15, 16–17, 18–19, 21, 22–23, 27, 29, 30 © Shutterstock; 13 © Wikipedia (public domain); 24–25 © Cracking Cavachons, www.crackingcavachons.co.uk.

Library of Congress Cataloging-in-Publication Data

Owen, Ruth, 1967–
 Cavachons / by Ruth Owen. — 1st ed.
    p. cm. — (Designer dogs)
 Includes index.
 ISBN 978-1-4488-7854-3 (library binding) — ISBN 978-1-4488-7907-6 (pbk.)
 — ISBN 978-1-4488-7913-7 (6-pack)
 1. Cavachon—Juvenile literature. I. Title.
 SF429.C357O94 2013
 636.76—dc23

                                    2012004524

Manufactured in the United States of America

CPSIA Compliance Information: Batch #B1S12PK: For Further Information contact Rosen Publishing, New York, New York at 1-800-237-9932

Contents

woof

Meet a Cavachon

What is smart, cute, has soft, fluffy hair, and huge eyes? The answer is a cavachon.

Cavachons are a **crossbreed** dog. This means they are a mixture of two different dog **breeds**. When a cavalier King Charles spaniel and a Bichon Frise have puppies together, they make cavachons!

Cavachons are small, people-loving dogs that love to snuggle up on their owners' laps.

Adult cavalier King Charles spaniel

Adult Bichon Frise

Cavachon puppy

Some breeds of dog have been around for hundreds of years. Cavachons, however, are quite a new breed of dog. They were first bred in the 1990s.

A cavachon puppy

People and Their Pups

Humans began training wolves and other wild dogs to be pets and working dogs over 14,000 years ago.

People wanted dogs to do different jobs. So, over many years they created different breeds by **mating** different types of dogs together. People bred dogs for herding cattle and sheep. They bred dogs that could track rabbits and lead human hunters to them. They also bred small, gentle dogs to be **companions** for people.

The first cavachons were bred in the United States. They were created to be companion, or pet, dogs.

Beagles were bred for tracking.

6

Border collies are bred for herding sheep.

Sometimes small dog breeds, such as cavachons, are called lap dogs. These dogs are happy to sit quietly in a person's lap, and they are small enough to fit!

A cavachon is a lap dog.

What Is a Designer Dog?

Some new breeds of dogs that have been created in the past 20 to 30 years are nicknamed "designer dogs." They are called this because **dog breeders** designed, or created, them from two older breeds.

The new crossbreeds have names that are made up from the names of their parent breeds. For example, the name "cavachon" is made up from the words "cavalier" and "bichon." Puggles are crossbreed dogs bred from pugs and beagles.

A cavachon

A crossbreed puppy can be more like one parent than the other in looks and personality, or it might be more of an equal mixture of both its parents' breeds.

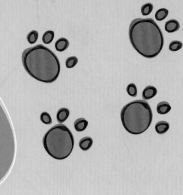

A beagle

A pug

This puggle looks like a mixture of its parents' breeds.

Meet the Parents: Cavalier King Charles Spaniels

Cavalier King Charles spaniels are gentle, friendly, intelligent dogs. They are good family pets and love to curl up on the sofa or on their owner's lap.

Cavaliers have a silky coat with wispy feathers of hair on their ears, chest, tail, legs, and feet. Their coats can be ruby, which is a brownish red color, or a combination of colors. These might include chestnut and white, black and tan, and tricolor, which is black, white, and tan.

Tricolor coat

Adult cavalier King Charles spaniel size

Height to shoulder = up to 13 inches (33 cm)

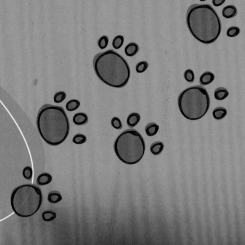

Cavalier King Charles spaniels usually weigh between 13 and 18 pounds (6-8 kg). They are known as toy dogs. This means they are a small dog breed.

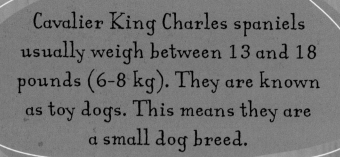

A black and tan cavalier

A ruby cavalier

Meet the Parents: Little Kings

Cavalier King Charles spaniels have been bred to be companion dogs for hundreds of years.

Cavaliers were the favorite dogs of King Charles I and King Charles II who ruled England, Scotland, and Ireland during the 1600s. The dogs were named after their royal owners! History books say that King Charles II was hardly ever seen without two or three of these little dogs at his feet.

During the 1700s and 1800s, the Dukes of Marlborough bred chestnut and white cavaliers at Blenheim Palace, in England. This coat color is known as Blenheim.

A Blenheim colored cavalier with her tricolor puppy

King Charles II as a baby
with a cavalier King
Charles spaniel

13

Meet the Parents: Bichon Frise

A Bichon Frise is an intelligent dog with a bubbly, cheerful personality. These dogs, often called Bichons for short, are very confident and love to be the center of attention. Bichons are bred to be companion dogs, so they love to be around their owner and human family.

These glamorous little dogs have a thick, curly coat that is usually white. They carry their fluffy tails curled up onto their backs.

Adult Bichon Frise size

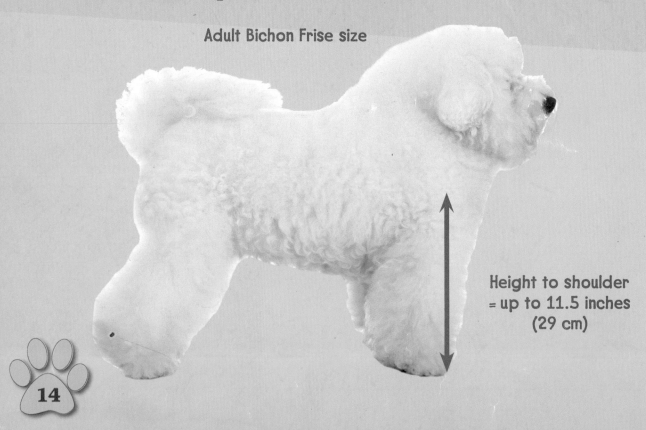

Height to shoulder = up to 11.5 inches (29 cm)

A Bichon Frise needs about 30 minutes of exercise each day. Its coat must be groomed every day.

An adult Bichon Frise

15

Meet the Parents: Popular Companions

Like cavaliers, the Bichon Frise has a very long history. As far back as the 1300s, Bichons were popular among royal families and other wealthy people in such European countries as Spain and Italy.

Because they were such fun to have around, Bichons also were companions to Spanish and Italian sailors. The dogs were so popular that their owners could barter, or swap, them for goods on their voyages.

Bichon Frise mother and puppies

In 1959 and 1960, two US breeders began mating Bichons. These dogs started the line of all American-bred Bichons to this day!

Cavachon Looks

When you look at a cavachon, you can see clues that its parents are a cavalier King Charles spaniel and a Bichon Frise. Cavachons get their coat colors and floppy ears from their cavalier parent. They get their soft, fluffy hair from their Bichon Frise parent.

A cavachon's coat can be peach-colored, peach and white, black and tan, or a mixture of these colors.

An adult cavachon usually weighs around 20 pounds (9 kg).

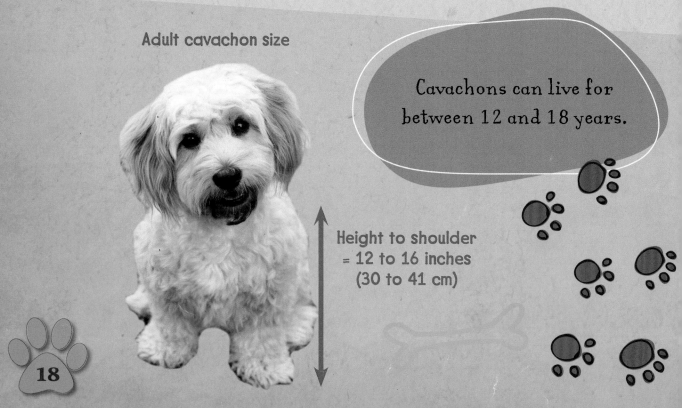

Adult cavachon size

Cavachons can live for between 12 and 18 years.

Height to shoulder = 12 to 16 inches (30 to 41 cm)

Cavalier King
Charles spaniel

Bichon Frise

This cavachon puppy is a
mixture of its parent breeds.

No Sneezing with a Cavachon

Many people sneeze or get ill around dogs because they have an **allergy** to them. Most dogs shed, or drop, lots of hair. The hair carries tiny pieces of dead skin called dander. When people with a dog allergy get near dog hair and dander, they may sneeze, have trouble breathing, and get sore, itchy skin.

A Bichon Frise doesn't shed its hair, and it has a low dander coat. People with allergies generally do not get sick around these dogs.

Bichons pass their low-shed, low-dander coats on to their cavachon puppies. This makes cavachons a safe pet choice for people with dog allergies.

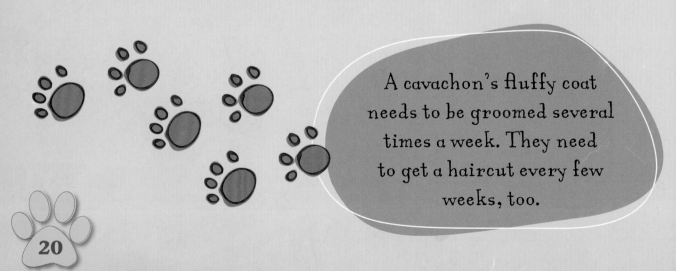

A cavachon's fluffy coat needs to be groomed several times a week. They need to get a haircut every few weeks, too.

Cavachon Personalities

Cavachons are a great mix of their parents' personalities. They can be full of energy and playful like the bubbly Bichon Frise. They are also gentle and sweet-natured like the cavalier King Charles spaniel.

Cavachons are calm, easy-going dogs that are never **aggressive**.

They take their job as a companion dog very seriously. They are always ready to give and receive love!

This sweet pup will grow up to be a gentle, loving dog.

Cavachons get along great with young children and easily make friends with the other pets that share their homes. Even cats!

Cavachons just love to make friends!

Cavachon Cuties

A cavachon puppy may have a cavalier King Charles spaniel mother and a Bichon Frise father, or the other way around.

The mother dog gives birth to a **litter** of around six puppies. She feeds the puppies milk from her body.

When the puppies are born, their eyes are closed. They don't open their eyes until they are about two weeks old. By the time they are four weeks old, the pups can walk, play-fight, and explore their home.

A Bichon Frise mother feeds her puppies

Like all puppies, cavachon pups need to stay with their mother until they are at least eight weeks old. Then they are old enough to go to live with a new human family.

An 18-day-old cavachon puppy

Designer Dog Puppy Mills

People who want to buy a cavachon puppy should make sure their puppy has not come from a puppy mill.

Designer dogs have become very popular. Some people want to make quick money by selling designer dog puppies. They set up puppy mills where the dogs are kept in cages in barns. The dogs are fed poor-quality food and may not get the medical treatment they need.

Puppies from puppy mills are often sold in pet stores. People buy a puppy from a pet store and don't realize that their new pup is unhealthy, or even sick.

Puppy-mill puppies have often lived in a cage their whole lives. They've had no chance to get to know humans and may be nervous and frightened of people.

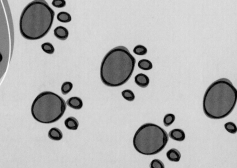

Buying a Happy Cavachon Puppy

If you want to buy a cavachon puppy, you should choose from breeders who raise their puppies in their own home. These breeders will be happy for you to visit their home to meet the puppies and the parent dogs.

Good breeders feed their puppies high-quality puppy food. They take the puppies to the vet to be checked for any health problems.

Little pups that start life in a loving family home are used to being cuddled and petted by people. They trust humans and learn that people are friends!

Puppies that are raised in a breeder's home will not be afraid of everyday noises such as the vacuum cleaner or washing machine.

Glossary

aggressive (uh-GREH-siv) Ready or likely to attack.

allergy (A-lur-jee) When a person's body reacts badly to something such as an animal or type of food. An allergy may make a person sneeze, get sore skin, vomit, or become seriously ill.

breed (BREED) A type of dog. Also, the word used to describe the act of mating two dogs in order for them to have puppies.

companion
(kum-PAN-yun)
A person or animal
with whom one spends
a lot of time.

crossbreed
(KROS-breed)
A type of dog created
from two different breeds.

dog breeder
(DAWG BREED-er)
A person who breeds dogs
and sells them.

litter (LIH-ter) A group
of baby animals all born
to the same mother at the
same time.

mating (MAYT-ing)
Putting a male and
female animal together so
that they produce young.

Websites

Due to the changing nature
of Internet links, PowerKids Press has
developed an online list of websites related to the
subject of this book. This site is updated regularly.
Please use this link to access the list:

www.powerkidslinks.com/ddog/cavach/

Read More

Hoffman, Mary Ann. *Helping Dogs*. Working Dogs. New York: Gareth Stevens, 2011.

Meister, Cari. *Cavalier King Charles Spaniels*. Minneapolis, MN: Checkerboard Books, 2002.

Miller, Connie Colwell. *Bichon Frises*. Mankato, MN: Capstone Press, 2007.

Index